Abingdon Elementary School Library
Abingdon, Virginia

TEST #5581
R.L. 4.1
PTS. 0.5

332
EL

A New True Book

MONEY

By Benjamin Elkin

This "true book" was prepared
under the direction of
Illa Podendorf,
formerly with the Laboratory School,
University of Chicago

Abingdon Elementary School Library
Abingdon, Virginia

Ⓟ CHILDRENS PRESS, CHICAGO

12656

Bank vault with paper money and bag of coins

PHOTO CREDITS

Don & Pat Valenti—2, 29, 40 (2 photos), 43 (2 photos), 44 (top)

James M. Mejuto—4 (top), 11, 13 (2 photos), 44 (bottom)

Hillstrom Stock Photos—©William S. Nawrocki, 4 (bottom), 9, 18, 22 (top), 27 (top), 30, 37, 39; ©Journalism Services, Inc. (Joseph Jacobson), 21 (left), 33 (2 photos), 35

Picture Group—©Philip Jon Bailey, 6

Reinhard Brucker—Cover, 15 (2 photos), 21 (right), 22 (bottom)

James P. Rowan—16

Historical Picture Service, Chicago—25 (2 photos)

COVER—Assorted coins of the world

Library of Congress Cataloging in Publication Data

Elkin, Benjamin.
  Money.

Previously Published as The True Book of Money, 1960

  (A New true book)
  Includes index.
Summary: Discusses the history of money as a form of exchange in the world and in the United States, and suggests things to do with money not being spent right away.
  1. Money—Juvenile literature. [1. Money] I. Title.
II. Series.
HG221.5.E428 1983   332.4   83-7436
ISBN 0-516-01697-0   AACR2

Copyright© 1983 by Regensteiner Publishing Enterprises, Inc.
All rights reserved. Published simultaneously in Canada.
Printed in the United States of America.
Original copyright© 1960, Childrens Press
   3 4 5 6 7 8 9 10 R 92 91 90 89 88 87 86

TABLE OF CONTENTS

Boys look at baseball cards being offered for trade or sale.
Even today bartering is done in many countries in the world.
The shepherds (below) are waiting to barter their wool at a market.

BARTER

Did you ever trade toys with friends? If you did, you were using barter. Barter is trading things without the use of money.

People have used barter for thousands of years. At one time, they did it at big markets. People came from miles away. They brought animals or grain or blankets or straw baskets.

The people traded what they had for things they needed.

People still use barter in some countries of Africa, Asia, and Latin America. They trade food they have raised or things they have made for other things that they need.

Market in Tunis, Tunisia

WHY WE USE MONEY

There is a true story about a singer who gave a concert in a country where people used barter. The people paid for their concert tickets with things instead of money.

At the end of the concert, the singer had 3 pigs, 23 turkeys, 44 chickens, 5,000 coconuts, and lots of bananas, lemons, and oranges. This was more than she could carry away with her—even after the pigs and chickens and turkeys ate the fruit.

It is not easy to do business by barter!

Suppose a baker wants to buy a car. With barter, he might have to give the car dealer many thousands of loaves of bread. What would the dealer do with that much bread?

People in most countries don't use barter anymore. Instead they use money.

A baker can sell his bread for money. Then he can give that money to the car dealer for a car. The dealer can use the money to buy other things.

Money is called a
"medium of exchange." It
makes trading easier.
Here's why.

With barter you have to
take what the other person
happens to have. Maybe
you don't need it.

When you exchange
money, you can use it to
buy things you need.

With barter it is hard to
decide on a fair price for
something. How many

Young girls sell pretzels to raise money for their club.

pairs of shoes should a person get for one cow?

It is much easier to decide on a fair price for something in money. Everybody agrees on how much a certain amount of money is worth.

With barter you might
end up with animals that
can grow old or get sick.
You might end up with
food that can spoil or get
stale. With money you
don't have these problems.

With barter you might
have to figure out how to
get three pigs and two
cows home. Then you'd

have to figure out where
to keep them.

Money is easy to handle.
It doesn't take up much
room.

People often raise
money for charities
or special projects
by selling tickets
for food, or
special shows.

KINDS OF MONEY

When we think of money, we think of metal coins or paper bills. That's what most money is these days.

But in the past, many other things have been used as money. Some countries have used cows or salt. Some have used tobacco, metal tools, stones, or cocoa beans.

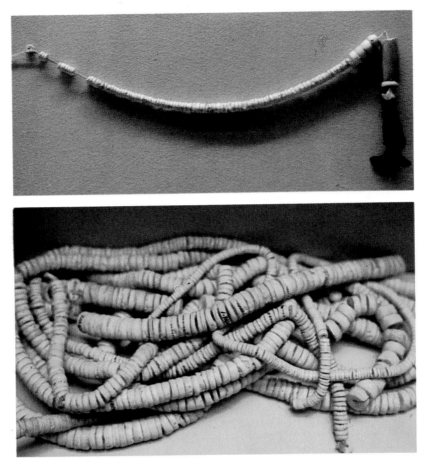

Examples of wampum

In early America, Indians used colored beads and shells for money. This money was called wampum.

Early settlers in America used tobacco, rice, and corn as money. They used animal skins, too. One time a governor was paid 100 deer skins and a county clerk got 300 beaver skins.

Traders bartering with beaver pelts

How would you like to earn that kind of money?

For a while during the 1600s and 1700s in Canada, people even used playing cards as money.

Historians think that the first coins might have been made in a country called Lydia about 600 B.C. (Lydia was where western Turkey is now.)

These coins were made of gold and silver mixed together. They were shaped like beans.

Other countries saw that Lydia had a good idea. They began making coins, too.

Ancient Greek silver coins used from 400 B.C. to 100 B.C.

The first paper money was made in China around A.D. 600. The explorer Marco Polo saw it when he visited China in the 1200s. He couldn't wait to tell people back home in Europe.

But the people in Europe thought paper money was a bad idea. They didn't see how anyone could believe a piece of paper was valuable. People in Europe didn't start using paper money until the 1600s.

Even today, different countries use different kinds of money. In the United States the "basic unit" of money is the dollar. In England it is the pound. In Canada it is the Canadian dollar and in Australia it is the Australian dollar.

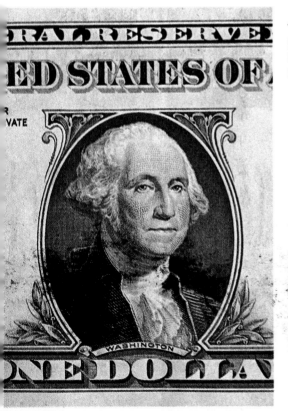

The face of George Washington (left) is on the American dollar. The Canadian dollar has a picture of Queen Elizabeth II.

A collection of banknotes and coins used in other countries.

Japan's basic unit of money is the yen. West Germany's is the mark. France's is the franc. Russia's is the ruble. Guatemala's is the quetzal. In Mexico the peso is the basic unit of money.

In New York City there is a Museum of Moneys of the World. In it are 75,000 different kinds of money.

UNITED STATES MONEY

Once each American
colony made its own
money. This caused many
problems. It was hard for
people in one colony to do
business with people in
another colony.

Then the United States
Constitution was written.
The Constitution said that
no state would be allowed
to make (or "coin") money.
Only the United States
government could make money.

VIRGINIA HALF-PENNY

THE BALTIMORE COIN

A PINE-TREE SHILLING

Coins made by three different colonies (left). The first
United States mint was built in Philadephia (right).

After George Washington
became president, the first
U.S. mint was opened. A mint
is a place where money is
coined by the government.

That first mint had no gold or silver for making coins. So George Washington sent a big box of his own dishes and candlesticks. They were all made of silver. Workers at the mint melted them into coins called "half dimes."

Over the years, the United States used many kinds of money. During the

A five hundred dollar bill printed by the Confederate States of America in 1864. It pictured the Confederate seal and the face of General Stonewall Jackson.

Civil War, the Confederate States even made their own money. When they lost the war, that money was worthless.

Today the United States
uses six different coins.
The largest is one dollar.
One dollar is worth

2 half dollars

or 4 quarters

or 10 dimes

or 20 nickels

or 100 pennies.

All these coins are made
of mixtures of metals. They
are made at mints in
Denver, San Francisco, and
Philadelphia.

Images on U.S. coins from left to right: Half dollar, John F. Kennedy and the presidential seal; Quarter, George Washington and the eagle; Dime, Franklin D. Roosevelt and torch and sprigs of laurel and oaks; Nickel, Thomas Jefferson and Monticello; One cent (penny), Abraham Lincoln and the Lincoln Memorial.

One cent coins have the picture of Abraham Lincoln on the front and the Lincoln Memorial on the back.

Coins made in Denver have a little D on them. Coins made in San Francisco have a little S. Coins made in Philadelphia have no special mark.

Each coin must show
the year it was made. It
must have the word
"Liberty" on it. And it must
have the motto *"E Pluribus
Unum."* That's Latin for
"Out of many, one."

Of course it would be
hard to carry money
around if it were all made
of metal. Ten dollars in
coins weighs a lot.

Abingdon Elemen...

So the government prints
paper money too. All U.S.
money, coin or paper,
carries the words, "In God
We Trust."

People accept and use
paper money because our
government stands behind
it.

Most paper money in the
United States is in the
form of Federal Reserve
notes. They are put out by
twelve Federal Reserve Banks.

Abingdon Elementary School Library
Abingdon, Virginia
12656

There are seven kinds of
Federal Reserve notes.
Each has a picture of a
famous person on it.

A picture of President
Thomas Jefferson (left) is on
the two dollar bill. President
Abraham Lincoln's face is
on the five dollar bill.

$1	George Washington
$2	Thomas Jefferson
$5	Abraham Lincoln
$10	Alexander Hamilton
$20	Andrew Jackson
$50	Ulysses S. Grant
$100	Benjamin Franklin

So, if you want a picture of Benjamin Franklin, all you have to do is get a $100 bill.

The United States government prints money very carefully so no one

Ben Franklin's picture is on every hundred dollar bill printed.

can copy it. People who try to copy money are called counterfeiters. The Secret Service tries to catch counterfeiters. Then they can be punished.

WHAT TO DO WITH MONEY

One thing you can do with money, of course, is to spend it. You can use it to buy things you need or want.

But suppose you have some money that you don't want to spend—at least not right away. What can you do with it?

You could hide it under your mattress. Or you

could put it in a can and
bury it in your backyard.

But those aren't very
safe things to do. So
people have found better
ways of taking care of the
money they don't want to
spend.

U.S. Savings Bonds

Sometimes they lend that money to the government or to a business. The people they lend it to pay them interest. Interest is money people are paid for letting someone else borrow their money. It's a little like getting paid rent for letting someone else use your house.

Sometimes people buy part of a business with their money. Each part

Stock certificates from different companies

they buy is called a "share
of stock." As long as they
keep those stocks, they
will get part of any money
the business makes. When
they want their money
back, they can sell their
stocks.

Bank teller waits on a customer (left). A bank sign (right)
tells people how much interest they can earn on
different kinds of savings accounts.

Many people put money
in savings accounts at a
bank. The bank works with
this money. People can
borrow it to build a house
or a factory. They can
borrow it to run a farm or
get a new car.

You can put money into savings accounts, too. It doesn't take a lot of money to open one.

The people who borrow the money pay the bank interest. Then the bank pays the people with savings accounts part of that interest.

Many people also put money into checking accounts at banks. They know their money is safe there.

Then, when they want to pay a bill or buy something, they write a check for the amount of money they need.

People often write checks to pay for the things they buy.

A check is a specially printed piece of paper. The person who fills it out writes down how much money should be paid and to whom. Then the person signs his or her own name.

It is wise to learn how to save money when you are young.

The person being paid can take the check to a bank and get money for it.

There are many ways to use money. Some are wise and some are foolish. Until you know a lot about money, it is a good idea to ask an adult to help you figure out how to use yours.

WORDS YOU SHOULD KNOW

barter(BAR • ter) — to trade by exchanging one thing for something else

coin(COYN) — to make money

check(CHEK) — a piece of paper used in place of money

counterfeiters(COUNT • er • fit • erz) — people who make copies of money that they want people to think are real and have value

Federal Reserve Bank(FED • er • il re • ZERV BANK) — one of the 12 banks that holds money and deals with other banks in its region

historians(hiss • TOR • ee • yanz) — people who study history

interest(IN • trest) — a fixed amount of money paid on a savings account. Also the amount of money you have to pay when you borrow money

market(MAR • ket) — any place where people gather to buy and sell goods or services

medium of exchange(MEE • dyum uv x • CHAINJ) — something (usually money) that people value and accept in exchange for goods and services

mint — a place where money is made

Secret Service(SEE • kret SER • viss) — a part of the United States Treasury that looks for and punishes counterfeiters

share(SHAYR) — a part of something one person owns with a number of other people

stock(STAHK) — something owned by a person that shows he or she owns part of a company or companies

trade(TRAYD) — to barter or engage in buying and selling goods and services

wampum(WAHM • pum) — shells strung together and used as money by North American Indians

INDEX

About the author

A former elementary teacher and principal, Benjamin Elkin has long been involved in the development of educational materials for young readers. This book about money was the result of a lesson plan Dr. Elkin developed for second grade students. Dr. Elkin has written beginning readers and served as consultant on several major language arts programs.

Abingdon Elementary School Library
Abingdon, Virginia

DATE DUE

FEB 1 0			
FEB 2 9			
MAR 2 1			
MAY 9			
JAN 2 6			
Cruse			
FEB 4			
OCT 3 0			

Abingdon Elementary School Library
Abingdon

332.   Elkin, Benjamin   12656
ELK   Money